PIECE WORK

PIECE WORK

poems by ingrid andersen

modjaji books

Publication © Modjaji Books 2010
Text © Ingrid Andersen 2010

First published in 2010 by Modjaji Books CC
P O Box 385, Athlone, 7760, South Africa
modjaji.books@gmail.com
http://modjaji.book.co.za

ISBN: 978-1-920397-07-4

Book and cover design: Natascha Mostert
Printed and bound by Mega Digital, Cape Town
Set in Garamond

Some of these poems have been published in earlier versions in:
New Coin, Numinous, Green Dragon, Botsotso and Incwadi.

Cover photograph is of Kaiser Wilhelm Memorial Church, Berlin. The window
incorporates salvaged glass fragments from the original church bombed
during WW2. (Photograph: Michael Andersen)

I was once told that one's closest friends in a lifetime can be counted on the fingers of one hand. This is for those feisty and honest women.

CONTENTS

FOREWORD

"Three years ago in Paris I got out of a "metro" train at La Concorde, and saw suddenly a beautiful face, and then another and another, and then a beautiful child's face, and then another beautiful woman, and I tried all that day to find words for what this had meant to me, and I could not find any words that seemed to me worthy, or as lovely as that sudden emotion. And that evening, as I went home along the Rue Raynouard, I was still trying, and I found, suddenly the expression. I do not mean that I found words, but there came an equation...not in speech, but in little splotches of color. It was just that – a "pattern", or hardly a pattern, if by "pattern" you mean something with a "repeat" in it. But it was a word, the beginning, for me, of a language in color..."

Ezra Pound, "Vorticism", Fortnightly Review, September 1914

It is a risk

To open up words,
unfold them to paper.

Found vowels,
hidden sibilants
chosen plosives

change shape
on a page.

Feat

My feet are the same.
Pale, unchanged,
marble, blue-veined.
Still slender:
their elegance
at odds with my body
in t-shirts and long skirts:
tired eyes, greying hair
and a thickening middle.

My feet are the clue:
flaunting spangled
beaded sandals,
rapidly pacing
a spirited, youthful
path with a vigour ahead
of the rest of me.

Waning

The moon's silver
has slipped into my curls.
Her shadows deepen
round my eyes
in lines of smiles.

The woman in the mirror
is more my mother than the child inside.

Away

The years the locusts ate away.

The spaces, places,
person she was,
the reasons she gave,
the shell she became.

The perfect wife.

Family album

I have
blank pages
instead of pictures
of all the things
grandmothers usually do.

I remember
her stiff blonde curls,
red red lipstick,
high heels, matching handbags,

fear.

Assault

I am slump-mouthed
in astonishment;
stutter-tongued.
You have, as I, a heart;
a pair of eyes, ears,
arms, legs.
You breathe and sleep as I do.

I cannot comprehend
this wild, mad anger
you fire, flaming, at me.
You frighten me.

You trebuchet.

Words

edge-on, like cards.
inscrutable characters.

words like
   anger
      hurt
         resentment
            conflict

take everything
with them.

My grandmother's chairs

It is hard not to think of you
while I cover layer and
layer of white paint
on your wicker chairs.

Your grubby
lies and manipulations
painted over.

Again

Like some obverse
of the sorcerer's apprentice,
I have flown
for long months, buckets
splashing,
filling your deep-dark depth,
breathing the seconds before the water hits
well bottom.

Inscrutable you.

Now it is over, I can see it.
I wonder how I could have done it all over again.
What defective gene or heart-scar drives me
to empty myself for careless men?

Bound

I hold white-knuckled to
ties from every side
binding me
to this life, this self, this now.
Feeling ropes pulling free,
bruising hands, twist by twist.

To open my arms
palms up, fingers wide,
to surrender the tensions
in which I stand

is unthinkable,
irresistible.

An inevitability.

The succulent winter melon

The succulent winter melon
lay halved
before us,
seeds brimming its middle.

How do the birds get to the seeds? you asked.
I suppose it must get broken, answered I.

End of a healing time

Sitting in this chair,
one of a listening pair
for the last time

after a year of drowning
in broken glass,
diving into my life
of your
love begrudged,
of words that slowly
sliced
away.

And somehow

I've come to this place
where the light is clear and gentle
where the words are
clear and gentle.

Good Friday

Meditation – First hour

I began the Good Friday meditation:
"Imagine Jesus walked into this church today.
What would he look like? How would you respond to him?"

Heads bowed, they didn't see Monica,
church cleaner back at work
her CD4 count up,
slip quietly in and take
her seat.

Eucharist – Second hour

You'd known that your
burgeoning plan
would need blood and pain
for fruition.
Your time must have drawn inexorably near:
the suffering, then the triumph.

Easter bells – Third hour

Good Friday's solemnity
draws to a close.

And the sacred
solid silence
of the stone cathedral
is suddenly broken, from the back

by peals of bells
and laughter
as an acolyte swings into the air,
flying, helpless,
joyous
at the end of the rope.

Shema

"My prophets and prophets," mourns the Lord.

His sad and weary messengers
who see,
who hear

and are not understood.

King Canute

King Canute knelt
on the shore
and whispered to the waves,
afraid their intransigence

would break him.

I am

I can almost feel.

So close,
I breathe your breath
speak your words.

I have the strength of redwoods
and fire in the marrow, this:

this sacred
anointed
now.

Doorway

It's quiet and peaceful here inside.
The flagstones worn to comfortable smoothness,
the rocker soothing in its rhythm.

I can see a triangle of sunlight,
like Vermeer,
clear-edged on the floor.

Gleam

The taut
round, red
gleam
of tomatoes placed across
the warm wooden grain of the kitchen table.

Their sudden haze of condensation
dulls the reflection
of light slicing
through the sash window.

Seduction

Steam lifts lazily
from the marbling milk
swirling
in my cup of morning coffee.

Here

The stream's murmured psalms;
the clear, worn earthen path;
the sacred leaf-green light
in the aisles and naves
of this
solitary forest trail.

Venturing

I'm making my way to you
cautiously
across this floor,
my bleeding feet
stepping
       warily
between
the shattered
       shards

of a porcelain vase.

I couldn't tell you

The silence now
that you've left the room
fills my lungs and
empties my mind
of all except
the thing I couldn't tell you.

Jabu

Your face is naked
as you unfold the detail
of your mother's fading,
erased by pain,
cancer seething beneath her skin,
her only desire
to die *herself*, with dignity.

My mouth is raw and empty,
this I cannot change.
And so you travel
on your own.

Message

She told the others
before she
could believe it herself,
breath held hard,
lips numb,
ears singing.

"They were too late."

He'd messaged friends
four hours before:

*I'm at the house
if u r looking 4 me*

Innocent words,
their meaning
left hanging
until they found him
when they returned for lunch.

left hanging

Violets

You don't like flowers
cut off
from the garden.

But you placed their faces
there to greet me
nonetheless.

Pieces

Amongst the whirled cones of small shells
and fractures of molluscs and pieces of stone
between my young fingers,

a tiny fragment
of china:
startling blue on clean white,
thrown up on the beach by a storm.

There were more over time,
fragile pieces
of clarity,
gathered and treasured,
kept together.

Some rounded, worn,
others new-broken.
Once, the whole
bottom of a bowl.

As a child, I'd imagine the sea drawing
back from the shipwreck.
I'd risk the water's return.

I haven't been back
for more than ten years.
I still have them. Now
I know how
to pattern my own.

Sewn

The stitch of silver
catches scraps of cloth
to card,
weds them edge to edge.

Years of contemplation, conversation
leave no record,
except these quilts.

Clean

Tall, ordered, dark
fir-feathered quills
write calligraphies of mist,
words of

repletion
contentment
saturation
peace.

Morning dew
on garden grass.
In mist's intimacy:
fresh, clean steps.

Kite

Black-angled wings
tip a solemn salute to the wind,
feather-stretched,
glide beyond me,
taking silence with them.

Days like these

On days like these
I eke my way
through the front door
sigh into a chair,
cold and hungry,
fact-saturated,
worn through.

A doorway for the visitors

St Peter's, Rhodes University

St Peter's building
has inverted crosses,
long halls for noisy orphans,
training and vocation
midst the swish
of starched habit and veil.

has bright bottle-bottom
glass fractures
and painted saints
guarding a door
most delicate
with rose and lily.

Miles away

Fridays, we meet unfailingly to escape:

are delighted, entranced or grieve
for those there briefly on the screen;

to meet the minds of writers miles away.

Siya on the London Underground

Bold in grey crowded silence,
you answered loudly into sudden hush at a halt:

"I wonder what it feels like to be ugly?"

Sparks of laughter lit the carriage long.

It's a physical pain

The stiff brown fast-food packet
I said I'd throw away, I place
carefully beside my bunch
of keys, between
the grey roots of the jacaranda.

I turn to wave farewell to you.

I feel red earth beneath my feet
still sticky from the rain the day before.
I take my time.
This is too hard a thing for me to do.

Home

The hollow of your shoulder,
warmth, spice of your skin, the
sound of your voice
within vaults
of breath in your chest.

Too soon

More than three years of
slowly settling self into this home.

Thick Victorian brick walls
breathe peace,
warm beetle-crazed floors,
patterned steel ceilings.

One hundred and sixty years of home are mine.
Mine is the secret cistern
seventy thousand litres deep.
The carved cupboard doors and dadoes.
The Settler roses, yet unnamed,
outside the front door.

All to end
with transfer papers and pen.

Lost

It's a strange grieving feeling, this.
Loss of home, loss of *own*,
huddled here in someone else's shell.

All is other: smell and space; the feel;
no place for familiar rituals,
books, papers –
no quiet space for fragrant, thoughtful tea
or poetry.

Coming of age

This space had moulded
itself snugly about the two of us.

Now you've woken, stretched
and flown,
leaving your castings behind:
withered socks,
gaping shoes on
the bathroom floor.

Your flight is higher,
your colours
are brighter than mine ever were.

How do I speak

How do I speak of this,
now you've gone?

All is well, all is well.

You've grown, you thrive,
man that you are.

I'm left with

silly, shamefaced sadness.

Sorrow slips

Sorrow slips into the day,
into days of countdowns, task lists,
phone calls, emails, invoices:
movers, prelims, finals, legal documents.

Softly, it calls low beneath
the sweetness of new love,
the promise of contentment.

Last times:
last autumn, Festival, winter,
but a month
left in this warm and graceful home,
like the ending days of pregnancy.

Clarity

Midst the scent of St Joseph's lilies,
rustle of tulle and taffeta,
new smell of your suit,
the clench of the ring on my finger,
murmured words

I realised you were wearing
the same old shoes.

A person

Abahlali baseMjondolo
affirms that a person is
a person no matter where
they're from.
Only actions are illegal.

But that's not always how we feel,
wait-listed and angry,
returning, work-clad, to
these shacks on borrowed land.

It's as if the zinc
has sunk into our skin.
We bear this shame
upon our waiting faces.

Batho Pele

Local government's
committed to process,
to committees,
workshops
that shift old stuff around.

Forms new fora
for stale strategies,
makes vague statements
in populist prose.

The elected elite
shun township streets.

They'd rather ask others
to flatten the shacks.

Leadership qualities

Familiar appointment criteria:
party credentials;
detention,
often without trial.

This assessment of competence:
is it
formative
or summative?

Never Again

For as long as I can remember, it's been
Lest We Forget.

Lighting Holocaust candles,
mindful of Rwanda, pogroms,
Bosnia, the Killing Fields,
necklacings in the next neighbourhood.

And now, this man,
burned
in our bright new nation,
unclaimed for days.

How does one emigrate
from the human race?

Burning the Fire Break

I'm called from my books,
this peaceful space
away from you.

The wind has whipped
the fire out
of control, it threatens the farmhouse:
all hands are needed.

I stand, armed with beater,
upon the border of veld and garden.
I think of *National Geographic*,
of fires in Australia, California –
I've not done this before.

Smoke burns bitter in my throat.
There. In the haze,
flames at the base
of the khakibos
in the close-grazed stubble
five strides ahead of me.

The wind behind them
suddenly shoves.

The fire flings up,
reaches into
longer grass nearby:
an angry wall that
spits and roars
towards me.

I face the flame,
stand firm.

You shall not pass.

Found Objects

Nobody cared when they were alive or mourned when they died alone. As more people live on their own, a growing number are dying unnoticed and unloved with neither friends nor family at the funeral.

There are a growing number of…modern-day Eleanor Rigbys who die with no friends or family to notice. Some have mental health problems and find themselves detached from the world. Some are elderly and have outlived their families. Sometimes there is no explanation: they have simply sunk without trace.

Around 200 funerals a month are unattended, a figure set to rise as it is estimated that, by 2010, 16 million people in the UK will live on their own. Where no relatives can be traced, the local authority pays for a basic cremation. Often the deceased's ashes are disposed of in unmarked graves. Their stories remain untold.

Elizabeth Day, The Observer, Sunday 17 August 2008
http://www.guardian.co.uk/society/2008/aug/17/communities.socialexclusion

Madrid – A man checking…a home he bought in a foreclosure auction walked into the living room and found the former owner's mummified body sitting on the couch, Spanish police said on Tuesday.

Coroners estimate the woman's remains had been there since 2001, when she stopped making payments on the house in the coastal town of Roses in the northeast Catalonia region. The body mummified rather than rotted in part because of the salty seaside air in Roses, a Catalan regional police official said, speaking on condition of anonymity.

The woman, in her mid-50s, was estranged from her children in Madrid and no one had reported her missing.

15/05/2007 19:39 – (SA)
http://www.foxnews.com/story/0,2933,272396,00.html

So neat, solid, self-contained,
this small box:
brown paper wrapping
with square, folded edges;
typed label
from a crematorium.
Heavy.
Too heavy for this space.

In Essen the decomposed body of a German man,
found seven years too late,
upon his bed.
Also his television guide, some coins
and a letter from welfare.

Police could comment that
no-one had reported
him missing.

A burglar in Berlin,
having broken into a flat
and found its tenant dead,
phoned the police and fled
without theft.
The 64 year-old man had
been dead for fourteen days.

Six months after I arrived,
I ventured to ask:
Who was this, bottom row centre,
in the church office pigeonholes?

It raised a memory:
Marie's struggle story of a bag of bones,
hardly ashes:
a man whose kinfolk could not pay
the cost of travel:

a burden that she carried in her car
for months after she had to flee her home,
until she buried them beneath a tree.

And the young woman that I met
by chance in Cape Town years ago,
in whose car glovebox lay a casket:
the ashes of her toddler
from which she could not bear to part.

Texas — As his family and neighbours in Beaumont, Texas, focused on rebuilding homes and lives battered by hurricane Rita, few gave much thought to Larry Euglon's long absence. "All the neighbours asked where Mr Larry was," said Osborne Johnson, who lived across the street from Euglon for more than 20 years. "We decided he had evacuated with other people and didn't have the chance to come back."

In fact, he never left. The skeletal, mummified remains of the 51-year-old recluse were recently discovered lying on his bed inside his home, which had no major storm damage but was still enveloped by thick branches from two splintered oak trees. Now people wonder why it took 16 months for Euglon to be found in this southeast Texas city. "I walked away with more questions than answers. You keep thinking why didn't someone notice this," said Jefferson County justice of the peace Vi McGinnis. "It has been the talk of the town." ...

His property gradually became an eyesore with overgrown grass and scattered trash, and was about to be sold for unpaid property taxes. A potential buyer inspecting the property on January 27 discovered Euglon's fully clothed body on his bed, atop the covers.

The interior of the house appeared undisturbed, covered by a thick layer of dust. The living room was still neatly arranged, and china plates and wine glasses still sat on the dining room table. ...

Johnson says no one is at fault for Euglon's death. "But we are at fault of him not being found," he said. "I fault myself because living this close to him, I should have called the police or somebody and had a search made for him."

14/03/2007 15:17 — (SA)
www.news24.com/News24/ World/News/0,,2-10-1462_2083123,00.html

No one could actually remember
when he arrived – it was years.
The funeral directors couldn't find a family.

For a long time he lay unclaimed,
and was sent on to the largest local church.
We hadn't held a funeral for him,
and he wasn't on our records.
They wouldn't take him back.

London – A British pensioner found dead in his bed is believed to have lain there undiscovered for two years, police said on Wednesday.

The body of Brian Dean, 70, was found at a terraced house in Accrington, in the north-eastern county of Lancashire, by police officers when they broke the door down. A pile of unopened mail dating back two years was found behind the door. Neighbours said Dean was rarely seen and was a private person.

Alarms were not raised with official authorities because bills were still being paid by direct debit from Dean's bank account. "We believe Mr Dean may have been in the house for over two years because mail dated back to June 2006 was stacked up behind his door.

"Mr Dean was a private man and it is very sad that he had not been missed by anybody for such a long time," said police inspector Jill Johnston.

06/08/2008 21:38 – (SA)
http://www.news24.com/News24/World/News/0,,2-10-1462_2371117,00.html

Edinburgh – The badly decomposed remains of an 89-year-old woman were discovered in her flat five years after she died, police revealed today.

Isabella Purves' body was only found after a downstairs neighbour noticed water dripping through the ceiling of her tenement flat and reported it to the local council. Officers forced their way into her flat, fighting through the piles of unopened mail which had gathered behind her front door, before making the gruesome discovery. It is thought nobody noticed Miss Purves was missing as her pension was paid directly into a bank account and bills were paid by direct debit.

Today, as detectives tried to trace the woman's relatives, neighbours, pensioners' charities and politicians spoke of their horror over the tragic case, described as a glaring example of the country's fractured society...

Little is known about Miss Purves, although it is thought she never married. The windows of her top-floor flat were left open today in the tenement building, which occupies a block on the busy junction with Broughton Road, above a pub and row of shops.

Last updated at 6:05 PM on 03rd July 2009
http://www.dailymail.co.uk/news/article-1197314/

Every day his presence
midst my messages and minutes.
Business unfinished.

Too weighty,
heavy,
waiting
in a graceless place.

*"Almighty God, by his burial your Son Jesus Christ
sanctified the grave to be a bed of hope to your people;
bless this resting place for the ashes of your servant
that it may be peaceful and secure."*

An Anglican Prayer Book, CPSA, 1989.

The retired priest and I
– then an ordinand –
met to lay the man to rest
under the green transparency of leaves.
We heard the children playing
nearby on their break.

a resting place:
a square cut clean in grass and earth,
cut deep through
white roots thrusting into soil.

Gritty, grey gravel, bits of bone,
emptied out.

Words spoken for a person never known,
a family we hoped
would have grieved.

Closed at last beneath
the peaceful churchyard turf.

E.O. Wilson believes we face the dawn of a new era, which he names after Greek ἐρῆμος (erēmos = uninhabited, lonely, solitary. erēmia = desert):

"The extinction spasm we are now inflicting can be moderated if we so choose. Otherwise the next century will see the closing of the Cenozoic Era and a new one characterized not by new life forms but by biological impoverishment. It might appropriately be called the "Eremozoic Era," the Age of Loneliness."

A word also derived from erēmos is hermit.

Consilience: The Unity of Knowledge (New York: Knopf, 1998), p. 294

Other poetry titles by Modjaji Books

Fourth Child
by Megan Hall

Life in Translation
by Azila Talit Reisenberger

Burnt Offering
by Joan Metelerkamp

Oleander
by Fiona Zerbst

Strange Fruit
by Helen Moffett

Please, Take Photographs
by Sindiwe Magona

removing
by Melissa Butler

Missing
by Beverly Rycroft

http://modjaji.book.co.za